Happy Birthday

Thank you for being the liquid sunshine that you are...

Rich Coming From Me

By Rich Butnotfamous

...and for helping me to think better of myself. May you achieve all that you seek.

Love,

Rd x

Copyright © Rich Butnotfamous 2016

The right of Rich Butnotfamous to be identified as the author of this book has been asserted by him in accordance with the Copyright, Designs and Patents Act 1988.

All rights reserved.

Create Space edition.

First edition

ISBN-13: 978-1537531267

ISBN-10: 1537531263

Photography by Rachael Clerke

Cover design by Ian Skriczka

Preface

This is a volume of some of my performance poems rearranged for the page. The difference in medium presents the opportunity to deepen insight and gain different perspectives into the topics I cover. I encourage you to listen to them as well as there is emotional weight in sound that a book may not convey, though binding the words in book form grants you the ability to dwell on what impacts upon you in sound as my pace is usually rapid. People often ask me to slow down to which I reply, 'Life doesn't slow down, how can I?'

The fundament to my word is consciousness, one quality of life that religion, science, philosophy and art consistently fail to explain and certainly something that I can't. You may well feel inspired by my blathering or fervently disagree. Either way, as a human doing poetry, I will have achieved my goal and that is to throw all into confusion and question.

You are a universe. Everything you perceive is your mind made incarnate. As the Torus flows, so too do we, dipping in and out of God's biggest practical joke that we call life. We can choose to heal and choose to hurt and have no choice but to do so. Archetypical for each other, blooming so that others may bloom and atrophying into the void again and again, love is the answer that is only one answer expressed infinitely. I am merely a humble mirror that you have created to challenge yourself on what you think and more importantly, feel.

Contrary to all evidence of your senses nothing exists here. You are the grand projector, so busy being yourself (which, by the way, is beautifully terrifying) you have to create seven billion versions of yourself just to do the taxes and the cleaning and that's not going so well is it?

You can listen to the performative versions of these poems here for free: **www.soundcloud.com/richbutnotfamous**

Contents

1. Rich Coming From Me – p9
2. The Planck Makes An Ant Look Giant – p13
3. Waspish – p35
4. Just Like You – p45
5. Where The Hell Are I? – p59
6. Wake Up Call – p73
7. For You Pt. 2 – p91
8. I Hate Words – p111
9. The Art Of Being – p127
10. Robotic Rise Is Prophesised – p135
11. The End – p145

Epilogue: For You Pt. 1 – p155

Rich Coming From Me

I'm Rich, but not famous
I'm Rich, but not bitter
I'm Rich, and creamy
I'm Rich, like a fine chocolate truffle
I'm Rich and nutty
I'm Rich, but I'd trade it all to be happy
I'm Rich, but wish I'd been born attractive instead
I'm Rich and therefore, according to the Tories, better than you
But having said that I'm Rich and according to Labour a bad person
I'm Rich and distinctive
I'm Rich, drinks on me!
...No, wait, I'm Rich but skint
Because I was Rich but I gave it all to the poor...
I'm Rich and full bodied
I'm Rich, but only in character
I'm Rich with friends
I'm Rich with knowledge
I'm Rich and aromatic
I'm Rich and can't believe I'm instant
I'm Rich for the day
I'm Rich because I'm miserly
I'm Rich, smooth and dark
I'm Rich, dark and fruity
I'm Rich and... fruity
I'm Rich but I don't let it go to my head

The Planck Makes An Ant Look Giant

Emptiness

A fizz
Pop
Whizz
Bang
In
Out
Up
Down
Left
Right charming son of a boson
An antimatter anthill
Out of kilter
By a
Proton in a billion
Since the

BANG

!

What was that?

The silent violent void
Makes particles paranoid
Of showing face in space
Where time is knot a plays
But a then
To now
To when
Venn diagram sham
Directing Dirac and Schrodinger's cat
To funny man Feynman
All lost on the layman
A chaos soup vacuum accumulating Higgs
Into hiccups

A planet pops in and out of existence every time
That you blink with your minds
I really don't have the time as
Already
Not
Now
Having
When's
Already
Having
Had
Had
Happening
Again

Einstein's playing dice with God now
Or not
Or has ag...
Look
The point is
Everything around us is going

WHEEEEEEEEEEEEEEEEEEEEEEEEEEEEEEEEEEEEEEEEEEEEEEEE
EEEEEEEEEEEEEEEEEEEEEEEEEEEEEEEEEEEEEEEEEEEEEEEEEE
EEEEEEEEEEEEEEEEEEEEEEEEEEEEEEEEEEEEEEEEEEEEEEEEEE
EEEEEEEEEEEEEEEEEEEEEEEEEEEEEEEEEEEEEEEEEEEEEEEEEE
EEEEEEEEEEEEEEEEEEEEEEEEEEEEEEEEEEEEEEEEEEEEEEEEEE
EEEEEEEEEEEEEEEEEEEEEEEEEEEEEEEEEEEEEEEEEEEEEEEEEE
EEEEEEEEEEEEEEEEEEEEEEEEEEEEEEEEEEEEEEEEEEEEEEEEEE
EEEEEEEEEEEEEEEEEEEEEEEEEEEEEEEEEEEEEEEEEEEEEEEEEE
EEEEEEEEEEEEEEEEEEEEEEEEEEEEEEEEEEEEEEEEEEEEEEEEEE
EEEEEEEEEEEEEEEEEEEEEEEEEEEEEEEEEEEEEEEEEEEEEEEEEE
EEEEEEEEEEEEEEEEEEEEEEEEEEEEEEEEEEEEEEEEEEEEEEEEEE
EEEEEEEEEEEEEEEEEEEEEEEEEEEEEEEEEEEEEEEEEEEEEEEEEE
EEEEEEEEEEEEEEEEEEEEEEEEEEEEEEEEEEEEEEEEEEEEEEEEEE
EEEEEEEEEEEEEEEEEEEEEEEEEEEEEEEEEEEEEEEEEEEEEEEEEE
EEEEEEEEEEEEEEEEEEEEEEEEEEEEEEEEEEEEEEEEEEEEEEEEEE
EEEEEEEEEEEEEEEEEEEEEEEEEEEEEEEEEEEEEEEEEEEEEEEEEE
EEEEEEEEEEEEEEEEEEEEEEEEEEEEEEEEEEEEEEEEEEEEEEEEEE
EEEEEEEEEEEEEEEEEEEEEEEEEEEEEEEEEEEEEEEEEEEEEEEEEE
EEEEEEEEEEEEEEEEEEEEEEEEEEEEEEEEEEEEEEEEEEEEEEEEEE
EEEEEEEEEEEEEEEEEEEEEEEEEEEEEEEEEEEEEEEEEEEEEEEEEE
EEEEEEEEEEEEEEEEEEEEEEEEEEEEEEEEEEEEEEEEEEEEEEEEEE
EEEEEEEEEEEEEEEEEEEEEEEEEEEEEEEEEEEEEEEEEEEEEEEEEE
EEEEEEEEEEEEEEEEEEEEEEEEEEEEEEEEEEEEEEEEEEEEEEEEEE
EEEEEEEEEEEEEEEEEEEEEEEEEEEEEEEEEEEEEEEEEEEEEEEEEE
EEEEEEEEEEEEEEEEEEEEEEEEEEEEEEEEEEEEEEEEEEEEEEEEEE
EEEEEEEEEEEEEEEEEEEEEEEEEEEEEEEEEEEEEEEEEEEEEEEEEE
EEEEEEEEEEEEEEEEEEEEEEEEEEEEEEEEEEEEEEEEEEEEEEEEEE
EEEEEEEEEEEEEEEEEEEEEEEEEEEEEEEEEEEEEEEEEEEEEEEEEE
EEEEEEEEEEEEEEEEEEEEEEEEEEEEEEEEEEEEEEEEEEEEEEEEEE
EEEEEEEEEEEEEEEEEEEEEEEEEEEEEEEEEEEEEEEEEEEEEEEEEE
EEEEEEEEEEEEEEEEEEEEEEEEEEEEEEEEEEEEEEEEEEEEEEEEEE
EEEEEEEEEEEEEEEEEEEEEEEEEEEEEEEEEEEEEEEEEEEEEEEEEE
EEEEEEEEEEEEEEEEEEEEEEEEEEEEEEEEEEEEEEEEEEEEEEEEEE
EEEEEEEEEEEEEEEEEEEEEEEEEEEEEEEEEEEEEEEEEEEEEEEEEE
EEEEEEEEEEEEEEEEEEEEEEEEEEEEEEEEEEEEEEEEEEEE!!!!!!!!!!!!!!

AAND

WEEEEEEEEEEEEEEEEEEEEEEEEEEEEEEEEEEEEEEEEE'RE

Not
Well, maybe you are
But
Physicists have no matter to grasp now pirates made them walk the
Planck
Length
Height
Width
Time
All in a rhyme
In a quantum
A what-um?
Sorry, a quanta
A quarter to three wasn't there third century
I see icy isosceles isolating exponentially inside a lullaby of lies
This vivid, violent version of inertia
A merger of fiction to fact
Shun the idea that anything's stable
You billowing cloud that's atomically fractal!

Observe
Uncertainty reigns in a place that takes pains to superpositionalise all
Life out of waveforms
A pebble dashed beach makes all of this uniform
Beans, Africa, gingham, a daydream
A Pontiac Firebird and mountain stream
A oneness
Cos all this just happened

Maybe

I'm still not really sure...

But then nothingness is an
Infinite
Schizophrenic
Immaterial
Epidemic
And it wouldn't be anything without you to see it
To feel it...
To hear, I raise a glass
For realities first class
A super tsunami positioning positive deposits of principles
Pauli excludes poor old time between electrons
HOW FAST ARE YOU?!

No, wait, where are you?

Oh, I see you!
You... weren't there a second ago...

...

That's probably the end...

Waspish

The Feng Shui
Of eschewing a wasp away
Tis a creature with which to play
As gargantuan
We are
To them
The small pain supposed
Fear enormously echoes
Like the cloud sheds its load on a tent

That poison a medicine to some
In Brazil it turns tumours numb
Can sir tenderly brush aside his plight
Confronted with barbs imbued with flight?
Afraid we are of such a pest
To rest in presence of luring scents
We bestow perfume to them
But fairer moans from wasps emerge
Where food is not
There comes a dirge
Of buzz in my right ear
And a hand of meteoric size and lumber
Bats away six legged winged venom

Phenomenal nests they build
Evolved to bees
Shrill parasite to some in fields
Yet whitefly they do subdue
For tomorrow crops they help us yield
As pupal irritants on wheat they infect

Insects that let us eat because they kill
Incept cockroaches
A hardy meal for their young
Excepting irritance when cider
They pilfer
And drown not in sorry weeping states
But confused as cans
They can't escape
Blind drunk from sips of sugar booze

The stripy bastard in throats has stung
One point on your person weak to swell
Suddenly turns picnics to alkaline hell
I can't breathe!
Quick!
Vinegar to soothe constricted pipe!
As stuck this creature drains my life!
Confusion is there to this end!
To cough it up makes no amends!
The damage done!
Trachea stung!
Precisely piercing breathing!
Lungs for air are screaming!
This happens it is true
Yet wasps like us are animals too
Their place to murder... justified...
Surviving death we all feed on life

And cleaning crops the wasps belie
A function in the Gaian might
In systems of our mother earth
Like us
Surviving in rebirth
These bits of planet whizzing round
Iron the blood
Lightning the mind
Pylons the trees of this future behind the design of a consciousness
Subtler than mine

And given this black, buttercup, aerial sniper
Can render a man to a boy with a swipe or
An aerosol assault against airborne assassin
A reflection is found in our cutting remarks
When we chide one another and leave mental scars
We sting and critique
We blame and we reign
In pompous
Self-import
Yet the wasp and all its family
Work better when in harmony
A lesson here then maybe
Is to lessen judgement softly
And dance with threat
And with risk

Regretfully, the comfort zone
Unless expanded shrinks at home
Discomfort with wasps can shrivel away
Just with fingers flamenco flirtation and being willing to say
"You're okay you know, actually, cos I see you in me
Another figment of a dream I live reflectively
And if you're in my presence I must've attracted
Attention to what my word means
When attack
Did I."

Just Like You

Just why
I don't see
Our sexuality
The originessence of our being
Is held
In secrecy
Until of age
We come to be
A child can understand
Human begets you
Man
Woman
Same
DNA mother and father are mixed
And balanced masculine, feminine traits and tricks
Of the trade
Held in shame
By tradition of dollar signing cock, tits and arse
But no blame
For a state of pure bliss
With loved ones

Remiss I would be to not fully declare
I'm a sexual being
Whole
Fully aware
That illusions of preferences, tendencies, tastes
Envelope our prejudice and pride
And lets rape happen
Where love should be given and shared
Not a mirror amongst you sheds no light on my bare
Soul

Where love for the self is dismissed as ego
A softness emerges
And raises its head
Not for show
But
Timidly curious, naked and scared
Til the abyss of this abscess permits us be bare with each other and say
'I FUCKING LOVE YOU!'
To everyone each day

What is it that keeps me from stroking your face?
Elevating this feeling that regardless of place
You've a union within you
Just waiting to bloom
Into humanity true
No it's not just a room
Or a cell that sells sextants to navigate shells of the sexual
It's an energy unpolarised
And I on eyes
Under scrutiny lie
Cos my gender illusory ripples inside
With the awareness of frequently stereotyping inwardly
Afraid of you seeing me
Just being me nakedly
Shamelessly humbled a human I am
Nailing self to the cross of
'What is human?'

The Adam and Eve metaphor
For
Division in self is to die for
Identity within, two become four
People evolving in the afore
Said mentioned parabola platonic cave with no door
Or retreat
From pornographic bleat

We are not teaching

Our children

They are beautiful

A little human microcosm taught it is sinful

Simply by being it is open to the wonder
Of a world all of their own in its splendour
The green
The blue
The muck
And you
Continue from the time you weren't
Alive until your end you've earnt
The credits roll on DMT purge
And where are you now?

This game set to hardcore
What is it I live for?
To grow or to shy formidable
Plans to escape the landscape I painted, more
Likely a blasphemy
About my own humanity
Will earn me a degree of hostility
Cos it's wrong
To enjoy
My own body

With every creature with plumage, antlers or wings
Lacquered, gnarled, piercing
Through skies eagles scream
And here I am saying
I can scream too!
I'm a human God damn it
Or bless it instead
Cos the world's full of people
Who enough have bled
For being born again into this school of the emotionally dead
So slay any notion I'm different from you
Being scared
Hurt
Or angry
I'm just like you too

Where The Hell Are I?

Right
I'm a diamond with a mind of facets and faces
Planes and imaginary places
Buuuut
I'm so shiny I can't find me
Periscope's up on the sub of marine psychology
Trying to peek at me behind me that's not me
Egads!
An ego!
Is that me or just imagery?

Hey, I'm great y'know
The 'real swell' aurora of comfort in which to dwell
The big chief
Head honcho
Top banana

Urgh
Do I sound like that?
Time to trim that fatigue
Oh
He's gone again...
Well he's me two
Twice the shutter speed
And in need of feed
Hungry bugger
Just like his

Brother

Waaaaagh!
Where did you spring from
Umbra without form
A total eclipse of the self!

I lurk round behind you
Where grim things excite you and...

Gods, you're worse than him!
This unhinged binge on the fringe of my borders has bored us to tears
The circumference of dark offence
Grows from whence
He goes and hence
Personas

Grow, we, the multiplicity and divisibility of
                Characteristics
              In which I stick
              I'd I.D. your id
        The bouncer on the door of club I
        Dent if I bash on the panel of me

Who's going mental
Cos really I can't tell
Where I begin
And you put the walls in!
Honestly
What am I doing in here?
These bits of my friends all make me a sphere
A ball and a party that rolls with the times
And on I roll with them
Invisible ties
And suits
Me to say what I feel inside
As mostly these rhymes come from not of my mind
Engendered instead by this Rich flowerbed
But wait
What is this opposite that across from me sits
A menagerie of femininity

Oooooh hello, cooo-eeee!
A softer set of shoes please and a hug that's a squeeze!
I'm the bloke in a woman and a woman in a man
Ooo that's a bit rude.

Well thanks for that bomb aunty me that's just great!
I took a left at the y and my 44 state
Seems to hide me inside shells of shards of the people I meet
And a mate that is more me
And the me that I can't see
Are just you in another me subjectively
So...
Where the Hell are I?

Wake Up Call

This world is merely my own mind I'm meandering around in
Manifestations of meyou moving through treacle
Treated to each other mes I am
When acting's a dance with the face
And loss of the self is replaced
By signs bestowed
Subtly by the low
In others

Isn't it odd that what we disbelievens out roundabout now?

Belief is just another word for love
Bankers for money
Junkies for drugs
Intellect you all a piece of the dream I'm having of you
My myriad mire mirror maze amazingly mimics my misbehaviour
Moreover memory's my mandatory modern day dream
Pretend you're me, right now, what would you do?

You see?

We're all each other, so let's just fuck...

Oh shit, wait, that's a different poem...

No actually wait, it is this one, so yeah, kinda want to fuck all of my
Friends
They're all meyou anyway, and why not to see
Their faces masks of ecstasy?

See now fourth dimensionally
Alive and dead you seem to be
So drawing from your memories
Of childhood is revelatory
In the sense that shame is your sunshade
Guilt is the beach
Nakedness frowned upon
Innocent speech
Sent to sway us back into the soft padded cell
Of a self
In the not now
But out of bounds

Namaste...

Have a nice day...

Hajimemashite!

Even on grey
Days
Each people you meet
In the street
Comes complete
With a you you haven't met yet
A requiem for the fear that keeps me appearing unsung in amongst all
Regret

It's all going numb
The world I mean
On the tube...
In Tescos...
Meyous made homeless from their own country
Meyou saw a homeless meyou the other day in the street...
Meyou was crying because it was so cold...
Meyou offered meyou some food but meyou couldn't eat it because
Meyou was pregnant and it was bad for the baby...
Meyou cried as well...

There are some meyous that abuse and infuse rules and views in
Meyous not me
Stop looking outside at the me that you see here before me
Use what's inside to unhide wholesome strategies
Wake the fuck up from this dream that you're not me!
And give love to every part of yourself that you're hating

In the beginning there was the word and the word was God...
Weyous' words

For You Pt. 2

You

You

And you

You love me

And I love me too

Because that means you love you too

And I'd like to see love in everything you are

And revel in the fact that you are who you are
Not him
Not her
Not them
Not us
But...

Inspirational
And fundamentally essential to exblisdence
As I know and love the turbulence
That rends the you
Out of me

How I'd love to say we
Illusionarily I feel the you in me
Gravitating through the yous I've met
Charm
Grace
Honour
Respected
Neglected
Clay wet
Yet still unset
Still I forget
All this I beget
This boomerang whirlpool
Of your world

Hurled I find myself amongst you
Pearled in agitation
And welling up with question
As to the validation
Of this emotion
And seeing gold
Still unsold
In your soul
And naked rebellion
Twixt
Your brain, heart and eyes flutter, not fixed
Nor need for repair
If ever was there
Unbroken
Untarnished
Not blemished
But relish
For my plate

And may I feast upon the you in me
This captivating, dark luminosity
All imagery in glances betray the ear in your heart
All bravery in chances abstain for fear of being hurt
Or indeed hurting that thing I love that's you
Damage being done to you
Done to me too
Through and through
This simple
Seductive
Salubrious
Umbrelatatudinaltruism
The schism reunited
The oneness of meyou ignited
Why fight it do I
And continue this lie
For the love of my life is that your life you love
As below so above
As within so without
No doubt...

Vulnerable
Venerable
You
A cosmic stew on which to chew
Holograms all in others' minds and dreams
A kind of stream
From which to glean
A glimpse of parts of me unseen
And dance do we, laugh, cry, smile and frown
Ecstatically you urge I dig straight down
Through muck and ick that writ my script
My autopilot mind that now breathes kindly
Not critically
For love I've found is all around
Bouncing back is this energy of me
Relentless positivity effloresces possibility to actuality
All back to me
And you
A living story rollercoaster node
So far from home and your abode
As I wrench you from that comfort zone
With words of love
While knowing I'm you
A DNA diversion down life's one way street excursion
A terminal of energy that may or may not know it's me
A version of the universe incarnate
Lennon now above said

"All

You

Need

Is..."

I Hate Words

I fucking hate words!
Obnoxious
Obsequious
Omnivorous
Oblivious
Ostentatious
Things we utter
Mental
Manifested
My mind makes more maps of moving mountains of meaning more
Overly stuttered
As I de-scribe
In the Latin, 'un-write'
My language picks apart the bits of things best left whole
Unspoken
Lest broken by my blather

What is a man?
Tall?
Forty?
Married?
French?
Black?
Matters not this lingual trot as round and back again thesauriously I
Espy a silence in this plight

Just

Stop

Speaking

...

With meaning dripping from loquacious lactation
Heartfelt meanderings of metaphors span a Milky Way expanse
Oxidised in sound and rust
No trust
That what I say hits home
You're a universe away from me, intimate proximity irrelevantly
Revered as to souls I draw near
Misunderstand my grammar plan
And fetch me a long weight, or paint, ta!
Tantamount to telling you
My words are mine
Each day anew the meaning deepens
The etymology of etymology, in the truest sense, the study
And remembrance of what words once meant
True now today, still, vagina et phallus
The sheath and sword mean division in people where genre's adored
As a label for genderfication

If I say the word rose
Can a flower suppose
In your mind?
Or does moving through air as you stood from a chair insist image one
Of a kind?
I can't tell you The Way
Doused
In Tao-t
When I say
Well
Anything really…
Confusion
Well, Zen
A budding layer often
Seen in jokes
When our humour words poke
Tragicomedy

Blispair in the air as we dare to share thoughts
Feels real as we peel away layers of sorts
Of the source of our sonority
Censoring subjects of sullen majority
Monkeys type Shakespeare theoretically in the face of all probability
But choose words I have to
To put across what I do
When we bathe in a fondue
Of verbs
Still…

I fucking hate words!

Crown a noun that can colour it right
In communicative ways out of sight
So much more is said
By the flush of your face or the eyes in your head.
Words can't come near to linguifying tears
The thousand dances of eyes always truth do belie
That is
Afraid might be I
Or elated or dreading my spells can misfire in your mind

And sentenced to life
In Babel's prison am I
With my cell mate the panda
It eats, shoots and leaves me, bleeding out on the sand
Of the language of England.
Although...

I fucking love words…

The Art Of Being

Close your eyes and imagine yourself saying these words...
This is not your world to protect
It is mine
Like experiencing every emotion in one motion
Me, the artist
Of my own life and exist
Tense with the same stuff as the Sun inside
Iridescent in ascent
And the dancefloor is mine
Until someone realises it's theirs
To whit...

A selfless place
Absorbed in now
And simply stating being
And then I
SiiiiiiiiiiiiiiiiiiiiiiiiiiiiiiiiiiiiiiiiiiiiiiiiiiiiiiiiiiiIIIIIIIIIIIIIIIIIIIIIIINNG!
Allowed I am to see
The world a self-recursive tapestry
Make and break
Rise
Fall
Spring into steps that I take as I glide now

A way to shake blame
Guilt and shame
The play of life's game
Voluminous rain on the tin roof
Give way
To the awe of this stage where we stay

The fire I admire in people beside
Me, is echoing thunder dust rippling wide
On the pond of my limitlessness and shhhhh!
The child in me is learning to be me again now
The monarchy inside so gleaming a castle bows
Samurai simply means 'to serve', lucid dream
Of the wizard is logic embodied in question
How joyous to give all I have!

Remember it's you that is saying all this
Though words are all ours
Ownership void implicitly here
I copied a baby by wailing in grief
Stole fire from heaven
Disbelief in a scream for the world and the hurt
And in brief
Saw the paradise lost until I sleep

And that I should do now
To let you be you now
Wherefore art thou, sandy grains on a beach or in stone
A willingness is now to make art
Part of home

Robotic Rise Is Prophesised As Cameras Come Alive

Photography
As the taxonomy
Of the momentary
Is academically
A quandary
As my eye to the lens
Lends a hand
To my memory
Embalmed that time upon a hill
Or in a zoo
Or in the chill of funerals for the now are held
In blinking, bleary glimpses
Save for silver nitrate rinses
Of photons
Reminiscences of partners past
Stir feelings now
That may elastic fast
My mind
To spring

That different me that does perceive
That once upon a time is me
Accelerated past the click and flash
Exhilarating, graphic lumen crash
Though sometimes this emotive cache
Bringer of the things dearly held
Tricks the mind
And serves to weld
Our present
To an optic trick

Though attached as I to that scene may seem
Snap happy missing captured days
As glued I am to screens so bright
Miss out on life
The framerate of reality
About 60 Hz not like TV
Hypnotic late night zombie state
Is flicking through the channels to sate
Searching for a fantasy
Of where you'd like to be

But I digress
A photo painting stunning is
With horse's legs displayed aloft
The ground, the stars and blood cells too
The beaming grin of silly old you
Of parents past
That romance last
A smile or frown may cross your faces
As places, people, pets erased
From here
Now are

That dusty album on the shelf
For forty years untouched for health prohibits the elderly
From reaching for those memories
Yet sons and daughters, fifty three
Assist in fetching bygone tomes
Of when a child they were at home
A paddling pool
That first bike ride
That bloody nose as from the slide
You
Fell...

Images fly around us now
1.8 million uploads a day... Wow!
The megabyte safe in the clouds is nothing
Compared to the millions of gigabytes letting you think
For now
Technology that we design
Swiftly evolving double time
Signs of our obseletion
As A.I. nears completion
To supersede the monkey gene
Or blend and borrow
Become tomorrow
Jogs my memories of TV
Becoming Star Trek in reality

Touchscreen a thing once sci-fi
Now home controls my hi-fi
3-d printing a face
A house
A heart
And chasing immortality
In the form of scientifically
Spelling magic materialistically
Instead of looking awesomely
At what we've yet to be
Not blankly beaming bemusedly
When suddenly the world goes
Beeeeeee...

The End

One day
You will be dead
It needs to be said
Maybe in bed…
Maybe no head…
Maybe you bled, either way one day you will be dead
Who's coffin up for the funeral?
What will they say as you spectate cremation of the space ship you
Once called a body?
Attacks on the heart leave a shell where the hermit's well groomed.
Though the loom of a husk from a

Car crash cos you were blind drunk in the pub and so deaf to the voice
In your gut
Now your belly rent open and face shredded I'm hoping a lamppost
You hit, not a child
I've seen a head bounce off a bonnet before
And a kid rise bloodied confused from the floor
He just ran out

Maybe a soldier you are
A life on the line
A towering God killer
The tiller
Of fields made of bones
In their own homes
Cemeteries amidst the trees of families eventually retreat back into
Earth
When time
The second it stops from chopping away at the trunk of your life
The scythe in the meadows of minutes
It exhibits no limit
To a babe born with cancer
African new born with aids
Nuclear mutations of humans and grave
Consequences of fear of the way
That we all have to play

An Italian ventriloquist
At a funeral his voice permissed
Him to chuck a groan into the coffin
The deceased to life he sprang and wife's heart of his did start to stop
A grievous comic incident
For murder
The performer now does time in the stint
What comedy in death!
The cruellest joke best seen vicariously
As nervously
To terms we come
By laughing away
How we'll exit someday

No more joy
No more pain
No more time
No more sight
No bills
No flowers
No criminals
No world
No sun
No war
No sense of that what you just did was an unbiased gift to the still
Living
It's gone…

Closing your eyes as you gasp your last
If you retain what is sane about you
You've done better than those in dementia's grasp
My gran was a vessel
Whose captain for eight years took leave of her station
Neither her nor her family familiar
Two strokes less genius
A brain tear and despair as her memories fell apart like
So
Much
Wet
Cake

As doctors prescribe to clinging on to such life
The danger is qualifying existence as just right
When no genuine smiles arise
Release from the suffering should be ushered perhaps
When identity fails and realities collapse
Or pain inconsolably clouds what's outside of its host
The guest of guessing mostly
When
Will
This
Just
End?

Although...
The warmth of this dream I consider my life
I feel adventurous despite this not knowing this land
With a cliff up ahead, and no parachute to hand
Does My Trying
Dying Mind Touch
Down 'Midst The
Distant Monarchal Theory?
Do mates of the soul reunite somewhat wearied?
Again quantum it tells us what Buddha's been saying
The rich void it makes us
And ferrymen need paying
Though I think by the Akron Family
It is better said...
"Don't be afraid, you're already dead."

Epilogue: For You Pt. 1
(A letter from my predator to myself)

Do you...
Do you want to call me a cunt?
Do you want to take a swing
And see blood fling
From my face?
It's easily done in any case, do it
This grin
Bash it in
Smug prick
Ever the clever Dick
You're so fucking weak
Looks bleak
Every time you seek
Love, tosser
You know I know everything you know and thought
Taught you not to love me too
About that knife you put in his back
That Queen taken by a knight
Not in your sight
And you just pawn in your castle, fucking rookie, die
Balls deep in shy armour amor n'est pas ici

Needle thin loneliness I am and keep you in the Nether of
Not fucking good enough
Utterly fucking pointless
A living fucking mistake
And this thirst is slaked when you fuck it up, AGAIN
That thing you call a brain in your fallacy
Lost in fantasies
Of conversations you wished you had, what's fucking wrong with you?!
I wanted revenge on you for loving me so badly I drew a sword out of
Thin air
Rapier to the point of stark outlook
Who'd choose you
Cunt?
Worm and slimy thing
Sidling long ways to allure
Alluding all to nothing as solitary hand solicitors don't dare to risk
Anything again
Are you even fucking listening?!
You're nobody inside somebody else's image of your ego again
The hollow shell she'll peel away if I'd let her

But
That's not my place...

Stay a while longer

Powerless

Don't lift a limb to sate that yearning whim

That rawness you keep quiet down low, that's me

That perversion
Diversion
You hide in the aversion
Of you
That's untrue
Is just glue
To keep you stuck
Pig
Every judgement you made
Kept you spayed
Bitch
Every heart you break cos you cower from love I frame in the dusty
Temple you keep forgetting

And it's too full

Dutch spring cleaning led you nearly full circle
A miracle
You weren't culled
Divine revelation
Left you in a train station
Of a ghost town no one can mention anymore
Tease
Who taught you that?
Where dy'a learn that dance
That screams romance
Left these lands
Cold and sandy?
Oh yeah, feel that shame
And let me blame
You for ruin in here
Hide inside a masochist sigh
Sure fire sign
You're far from fine

Loser

Lonely

Lost

Clutch and grasp the thread that's leading you round again
Maybe this time the chilli will be sweet
Ha
Yeah
Sure
Every time you get it you lose it
I'm keeping it here in hell for you
It's ringing alarm bells again in you
Yet you keep missing the stop
And hop on again
Flailing yourself now
As all I have to do is laugh
And you break

Oh, all that are you?
Turn your hand and it gets good
Only impresses you and should
It come to pass on by
You just tell truths disguised as lies
By speaking simply with your eyes
How terrified you really are

Not far now
Not much left to say
Only disappointed disrespectful jibes I jubilantly wrap round you like
Anaconda manacles
Writhing anaesthetic mind I shine to actually keep you safe
Don't risk anything

I
Your quadriplegic liege do leer and smirk in your shadow when you
Trip again
Self-inflicted affliction flickers neon in your own snide snipes at others
And mirrors down deep within you
You gave me this power by being
Regardless how much you sing
I can't leave you
Always and never I am
At least if it's dark in here
I
Can still keep an
I
On you

Made in the USA
Columbia, SC
12 November 2017

Made in the USA
Columbia, SC
12 November 2017